Where Darkness Meets Light

A Poetry Collection
By Sabrine Elouali

For all of those who struggle to find the light.

I had always wanted to write a book of my poetry. It was one thing on my bucket list I swore to myself I would do one day and finally that time has arrived. I feel ready and raring to go. I have never really been a huge fan of my own work, or of anything that I do, but I'm willing to put this out there for the entire world to see, not for myself, but for others. I know and hope that my words will reach someone in need of them. I don't have all the answers, heck I'm still looking for them myself on a daily basis, but I hope that something I know, have seen or experienced may help someone out there who needs these words to find comfort or peace in an often messy, hectic and overwhelming world.

Decisions.

When it comes down to that one crucial moment,
Where you stand on the verge between right and wrong,
When time is a privilege you no longer have,
One or two words depend on the fate you endure.

"I didn't expect it to be this hard"
How you realise if you make the wrong move you find yourself
down the incorrect path.
A decision creates a barrier between you and sanity,
As it eats you alive, you find yourself vanishing.

Hmm..

When daylight breaks, I lie awake,
Between thoughts I breathe,
From my home I cannot leave.

A cry like shattering of glass,
But what will be of my broken heart,
A nightmare that's real, can that be so?
I try to distress that the answer is no.

When alone and cold, I turn to myself to hold,
Through blurry eyes, I try to see,
What has become of me.

Blur.

In Front of eyes, just murky skies, it seems to be
Standing still - time.
Never i thought, would be so lost,
Like treading away through endless moss.

Is everything I believed a lie, it never ceases
To make me cry.
I think of everything that's gone, in the race
Of life I'm clearly getting bronze.

Now, I lie in wait for the day,
That this will all be whisked away, everything was
Nothing but a nightmare.
But wait. You don't even care.

To continue.

To and fro this world i roam,
Up - down, all alone.
Everything moves so slow,
Like the first falling of winter snow.

Do you see me yet my friend?
It feels like a world is coming to an end,
My heart is in urgent need of mend,
Happiness, please give me a send.

To look upon you, it gets harder,
I don't know if I can go much farther,
Will there be an end to this fearful show?

'Cause a wall is blocking the ever-dimming glow.

Passing time.

Staring through a shadowed window,
Watching the blue sky turn to grey,
Seeing seedlings sprout atop a muddy gutter,
And the laughter rushing past.

The evil looks and metal bars,
The hardening stairs and dirty floors,
The gravelled ground looked at from above,
And the creases on my shoes.

Awaiting the bell to chime,
The wind purring outside,
They don't see me.. I see them,
Just another lonely day again.

Prevention.

A spark turned into a roaring inferno,
The dwindling of sanity, a distant glow.
The possibilities seem endless,
Thoughts, racing, never rests.

A pace beginning to increase,
Like a dog, violently wriggling from its leach,
Remove the thoughts from your mind,
Don't let it dissect the panic up from inside.

Questioning.

The watchful eyes of an unknown source,
This has been the case for years, of course,
Staring, reminiscing, breathing hard,
Are you living on a fading battery charge?

Do you remember, how it felt, how it meant,
Nothing but teeth tightly clenched,
Pictures, smiles, a love train,
The images flooded with teardrop stains.

What if, if only, how, why, questions galore,
An abyss slowly dragging you down to the floor,
Hold on, fingers slipping, hope shrinking,
Just be strong.

Is this marking an end to a life long song?

I don't know if you know but..

His voice bellows through an empty hall,
Barely there to answer a call,
Why was it like this? I ask,
To think about it is a daring task.

No emotion, a blank page,
His spirit seems to grow with age,
The purple, blue and orange,
Seems to be the most important to him.

Tales being told, just shattered glass,
Is everyone seeing through his mask?
Piercing through and tearing up,
What ever happened to the love?

A Joke I'll Never Get.

The funny thing about you
Is you speak with flowers and thorns.
You appear underneath a halo
But it is only to hide your horns.
If someone dares to say against your words
Eruption surely follows.
All the lies concealed as soft promises
Tear through the delicate membrane.
And who to fall victim to your wrath
Than the same as years gone by?
Knocked down and out for the count
But you're ambivalent..
Time moves and you persist,
Long gaps of thumping silence.
Your voice slips in
Seems you forget where the wounds are
Back around to the start
Were I must now re-write the words
Because the funny thing is,
It's not funny.

Toxic.

Like nicotine coursing through veins
Restricted and still - tied in chains.
A warning that forever foes ignored
Faith that one day you'll see your approach is flawed.
Subtracting time from an invisible face
Without a shot feels out of place.
It's plain to see you are poison
Now with will I must ignore my mind's noises.

Nothing Is Futile.

When will you realise they're not thinking of you?
Perhaps you were never part of their memories to begin with.
You can reach out and take as much happiness as you decide;
Unless you passively await rescue as your life trickles through a sieve.

Simplicity.

There is little if any need to make this so complicated.
Causing your own logic and judgement to become faded.
The sooner this is realised the better.
Let go of the crutches and the hands you rely on - go for it unaided.

D&L.

This won't be like times before.
This can't be like times before.
The circles you've grooved around yourself cannot go any deeper.
The English language has only a finite amount of excuses.

It can't be laid on another's shoulders.
It won't be masked as success without it being so.
The chances could have been taken -
Now is redemption, no take two.

What Now?

I didn't think it took that level in order to be amongst you.
And although the actions can imitate - they never feel true.
Hidden away beneath clouds of dark and behind locked doors.
Nothing but the incessant forcing of an idea "the choice is yours"

What conjures in your mind is half the battle, but structure collapses without consistent building.
To stop and hold, to convince oneself it's all just a feeling.
Words on a page provide clarity, but yet stay incomprehensible.
What lines can be spilled out now - they all remain indefensible.

Such a simple equation, but outward complexities.
No longer a want but a desperate need.
Even when the answers lay within your hands and heart.
False beliefs and fear struggle to part.

A Week In Solitude.

This day looked much like the one before,
And this one followed closely.

This one seemed to offer a change.

But this one returned old ways.

This day could hold me frantic and confused.
This one tends to share itself with others.

And this one scares me most of all.

Those Games You Play.

When will these thoughts halt,
Each syllable presents strain.
To realise and ignore is a lesson must be taught,
But how does one dissect the engrained?

In every twirling teacup lives a sea of words,
Even with delicate manoeuvre the liquid leaps out.
Through the ears the same help goes yet it is never heard,
Each sentence and picture presents just more doubt.

How can things sink so deep and so fast,
Time dragging you along as you remain stuck.
Everytime it is sworn that this occasion will be the last,
Then another load of negativities arrives in an unwelcome truck.

Does all this help or is it simply here,

Does anything feel worthwhile,

Is it nothing but suffocating fear,

Is it all just worry and denial?

New Patterns.

Rail tracks that lead the same way.
Surroundings ahead and behind - all the same.
A factory line pumping out copies.
Yet despite their defects.
The same force that had been present from the start.
Observing now through another lense.
A track on diversion.
A destination of choice.
Seeing past familiar bushes and overgrown paths.
Arrival to the beginning, nothing changed.
And yet everything has.

Total Summary.

All the excuses, all the words that don't make sense.
All the lies and twisted tales, all the feelings just tense.
All the mixed up pictures, all the memories skewed.
All the stress and pain, all the things you "have" to prove.
All the fears and the panic, all the anxiety amplified.
All the days wasted and time passed, all the ways it can be simplified.
All the false beliefs and nonsense, all the logic that has none.
All the defeats and the surrenders, all the times you could have won.
All the space ahead of you now, all the clearance to do.
All the lying clouds and thundering noise, all disappear from view.
All the signs that were presented, all the truths that are told.
All the things that can be done right now, all yours to hold.
All that needs doing is to see from another's perspective, all is there on the surface.
All the reoccurring thoughts and same old stories, all try to make you nervous.
All the time in the world is slipping through, don't forget and be ambivalent.
All the good things you see and the things that are done,

All you need to know is you are not different.

Blocked Connections.

I can feel you through electric walls,
Even when the world becomes stalled.
Your presence still fills my space,
Though you may be miles away.

You cry and I'm calm - I seem strange,
Do nothing but remain trapped all day.
Funny thing is, after years this is comfort,
A place to hide when my mind is submerged.

Self Belief.

You've seen the truth many a time,
Only getting down to the subconscious mind
can stop these lies that hold you back,
Can release the bright beams from the black.

Patience it'll take and strength of self,
All along you were your own help,
Take small steps but take them firm,
Without going through discomfort - nothing learned.

When the negative patterns flood in again,
Don't be convinced they're a friend,
Don't sink into that sand once more,
Don't be dragged down to the floor.

Nothing would have nothing will,
And to believe in that will take skill,
But once you can know it's all false anxiety,
Only then you shall be free.

25 Words.

Sometimes we feel
like more Is better.
Exaggeration
Effort
Eccentricity
Essays
But we could boil it
all down to its simplest form.
Still remaining enough.

Crowded Rooms And Empty Paths.

Began as calm; uncertainty, shifty eyes,
Self conscious and analytical.
Tempo changes, heart rate ceases,
Switching between clenched teeth and smiles.

Words on a non existent realm told more truth than mouth,
Every step was agony with pain in each move.
Trying to direct attention and think clear as could,
Falling in and out of thought, wondering each time.

Just a small thing; ''twas awkward but honey,
Deciding where your mind stood was a puzzle.
Down an encased space to arrive at somewhere new,
Crisp air and cold gusts were about to suddenly change.

One look with shining eyes,
Touching feeling; is this wise.
Not knowing where to place,
A hand a nose upon face.
Breathing quickened,
Muscles tightened.
Considering and moving closer,
Hands moving ever lower.
Both wanted to see, then there,
Now sharing breath not breathing air.
Slow pace changes fast,
Was I right? What a task.
Grasping at skin and hair,
Just going full without a care.
Back inside the box we began,
Not sure what of a plan.
Questions fluster; they surround me,
Radiating absolute anxiety.
Was it what you wanted; was it good,
Did it fulfil everything you thought it would.

But..

What if it is all the stories you told yourself.
Deepening grooves like embossed patterns within your mind.
And everything you held as belief can fall apart instantly.
What if you had perfect vision when you stumbled around as blind.

What if it is all a waste - energy poured into destruction.
All the endless cycles that made hours feel like minutes.
And the possessions that trickled away.
What if you actually believed the evidence, even just a bit.

What if it is all just space and time flushed down the drain.
Do you think you'll make what you have left what you want?
Like others it's not a question.
What if you held power all along, but only felt you don't.

Going Down.

Grooves like a stuck vinyl
Patterns of tiles
Or copies of files.
Jerking disc jockey without the fun
Replay button used more than once
Each time you should be done.
Heart racing in and out of time
Overwhelmed - you can't hide
Questions fill inside.
Follow trails of misleading novels
What a task to have
Lorry loads of worry, continuous drag.
Somewhere on this line
No more "belief" shrines
Cut the false rope that binds.

Years Of Scripts.

Nothing happens if done or not,
No difference whether it is crossed.
Each time the same threat presents,
Completely held under false pretence.
And yet those days pass as they do,
Still belief in what isn't true.

What does it take to see past?
Just built up excuses, constant "cants".
How can it be that this theory is not yet destroyed?
Even when it only exists in your mind -
null and void.

Mountains of pages filled with evidence but still not enough trust.
One way to go to free yourself,
Not a denial, it'll feel like hell.
But faith in reality will pull you through,
Finally doing that you thought you'd never do.

The satisfaction now is deceptive,
Sucked right back into the repetitive.
Look back at time that has gone so fast,
Look forward and see the same pain last.
Insane to think the small is insignificant,
You've proven to yourself that deep falling is evident.

When the moments arise - ignore the now
Pass by they do like clouds.
An internal alarm malfunction,
Recognise it's broken when at each junction.

That which it makes you feel is lies
Simply covering up the truth inside.

Pure Imagination.

It's actually an asset, a gift to behold.
Use it well and do wonders you're told.
But it chooses to run riot, tornados swarm.
This part of it was never warned.

Taking hazy photographs - they're multiplied.
With complete disregard for space and time.
The ghosts smother this present world.
Stood feet dug in place with toes curled.

Turn the enemy back into an ally.
Keep it in line without unnecessary cries.
What's done in evil can be done in good.
Retrained to behave as it should.

Then the dust settles and air calms.
Even stars shine - the lights dance.
Now only a single projection can play.
Showing dreams and joy till your final day.

Anti socially social.

You're not wrong for needing space.
No need to exit your sanctuary with haste.
Let yourself breathe and gather your thoughts.
Allow solitude to show what school never taught.

Regurgitate.

Some days I didn't know where to start
These words like pulling teeth.
Yet the irony was not lost on me
That my head be so full.
Clasping at some kind of inspiration
Amongst the myriad of conflicting thoughts I hold.
And nothing feels right
Nothing feels adequate
And nothing feels good enough.
Much of art imitating life
The confusion and disarray
The constant frantic heartbeat pattern of being.
"Where was this going?" I asked myself
Much the same answer as I pose every hour
Trying to salvage through the mess
The turbulence
The deafening ticking of every clock that surrounds my environment.
I touch the screen
I sit and think
I clutch at straws as they trickle between my fingers.
To and fro
This way and that
Some days I don't know where to start.

Sceptic.

Call me a sceptic,
Call me insane,
But don't dare question my thoughts
When you've not felt my pain.

Solitary Confinement.

When all is said and done -
What could we say?
Would you regret your decisions and your lack of actions,
Isn't that what adds up at the end of the day?
Now it seems everyone looks for someone to latch on.

When all is said and done -
We just don't know.
The overwhelming pool of clichés we drown in.
Would we kick ourselves for going to and fro,
And go forthwith without question.

When all is said and done -
Will anything change?
Because we've been forced to reflect on it all.
Do we now take it on our own backs, the blame,
Or would words be spoken to a concrete wall?

When all is said and done -
We can make this different.
It seems ignorance can only be overcome when presented with death.
Will we finally seize the moment?
And savour every one of our breaths.

Divide.

It was no love affair
As been presumed.
No honeymoon phase
Or beautiful flowers in bloom.
It was hostage
Held under sophisticated ways.
No one counting
But an endless amount of days.
Patience did nothing
It had to come from inside.
All she wanted
Was for them to divide.

Questions.

Why do you sabotage yourself so?
How is it you can know everything required and yet be trapped?
What ever happened to knowledge is power?
When will you be able to wake up to the world?
Where do you see yourself if you allow this to destroy you?

Why do you not believe in the power you hold?
How do you expect to change whilst repeating the old?
What do you want from this life?
When are you hoping to start living your years?
Where will this darkness lead you?

Why can you not accept what's staring you right in the face?
How do you listen to such a thing that doesn't exist?
What are you going to do now, do next?
When will you start because time doesn't stop?
Where do you want to go in this life?

Why do you diminish your strength and distrust your logic?
How has this been escalating so long?
What will stop you from touching that again?
When are you planning your life to begin?
Where are you currently going, is this what you want?

Why can't you take that leap and see what you knew?
How have you let your days slip away?
What change can you make now that will help you tomorrow?
When, if ever, will you actually be "ready"?
Where is your mind right now, check yourself?

No matter the amount of words.
No matter the volume of intelligence.
If you don't do what you don't want, you can't do what you do want.
This is the fact you must accept.
There will never be an alternative route.
No shortcut.
If you run now it will still remain later.
Nothing changes unless you change.

A Serial Offender.

How can it be so predictable yet utterly startling,
Almost running like clockwork - right on schedule.
Acting in surprise at the turmoil it brings,
Once again clouding you with all that's untrue.

It enjoys watching you at the mercy of it,
As a cat with a mouse, let go and pulled right back.
Why can't you dismiss it again; it's the same old trick,
Compose yourself, calm down, get back on track.

Those fleeting moments of epiphany - keep them close,
Avoid the trap it places in your way.
Stay steadfast to the reality your soul knows,
A familiar darkness, don't let it lead you astray.

Alarm.

What was it?
That noise amongst the silence
Amongst the hustle and bustle
The agonising groan hidden in the distance
The constant ticking
That air raid siren only you can hear
That screech on a chalkboard
There's no off button
Just your own internal alarm.

Illusion.

I don't think there is another as frustrating,
As the soul of a person endlessly chasing,
Like a confused and frantic dog to it's tail,
Round in circles continuing to fail.

To be such a prisoner in a world of freedom,
Yet going against your mind is surely treason?
Knowledge enough to fill countless books,
And still from these invisible shackles - you can't be shook.

One cannot blame what is blatantly there,
Seems to the outside world you just do not care,
Though nothing be further from the truth,
My goodness if they only knew.

There is but a single way out,
No other options; no need to look about,
Take all those thoughts and toss them aside,
Muster any ounce of courage from inside.

And what's terrifying is the days will roll on,
And you and I passively wait to feel strong,
And we'll look back to hate that we were trapped behind that wall,
And we'll hate ourselves when we realise we were never stuck at all.

False voices.

The words heard are not you and you are not them.
Stepping off the spinning top presents the solution.
Placing a hand within your own holds more than once thought.
No longer suffocated behind a wall of pure delusion.

A Glass Bridge.

I stumbled through the darkness,
Attempts to grasp at light,
Embarrassed at my unsteadiness,
An invisible opponent to fight.

Despite laying my feet on solid ground,
I see a broken walkway beneath,
To shake from delusion - not allowed,
Embedded programming I need to delete.

Moments of reality flicker through,
Behind opaque glasses my eyes
cannot see what is truly true,
Leaving them smashed on the floor below is where truth lies.

Seesaws Were Meant To Be Fun.

Like opposing forces
Repelling magnets
Tug of war with no winner
An internal struggle to not repent.

Multiple dendrites with no known end
Pitting fire against water with a magnitude of force
From an oblivious window all is calm
Like fairground pop ups are the thoughts.

Where do we meet resolution
When the conflict rages on
All attempts to avoid it
The fear of choosing wrong.

Lockdown.

What was once thought to be fiction,
A mere human imaginal depiction,
Now encircles this existence,
Despite attempts at resistance.

A vision of tasks and goals aplenty,
But all require the liberty to be free,
A complete downward detour unexpected,
Scoffs and laughter as all plans rejected.

At a time when everything is inverted,
Impatient civilians question is it worth it?
Where the irony to do the easy and plain,
Is now what's most difficult and drives us insane.

But surrounds us are signs and glimmers of hope,
Showing heart warming side effects to keep all afloat,
Despite the chaos and fear that ensnares,
As a collective we become more consciously aware.

Who knew we'd be amidst a marking in history,
One that perhaps never again to be seen,
What we've been given a blessing and a curse,
An awakening to humanity to save this earth.

Swords edge.

You can't wait for it.
Time passing, yet you're still.
Trapped in a dark delusion.
Shackled to a chain that doesn't exist.
The door is open, though it appears locked.
Fearing the voice that speaks impossibility.
You are what creates your reality.

Would You Rather?

I'd rather not do that again,
I'd much rather do this instead.
I'd rather not reinforce those things,
I'd much rather avoid the pain it'll bring.

A toe tap or hand touch,
Turn around so they don't watch.
On again and off once more,
Think I'll just let it cascade onto the floor.

Tracing memories and replaying hurt,
Is it not better to remember my worth?
Buying into facades and illusions,
This time I know they've had their conclusion.

I'd rather not lay in darkness,
I'd much rather do things that require a harness.
I'd rather not be a prisoner within my own mind,
I'd much rather see the clarity after years of colourblind.

No.

Be gentle with yourself
Be patient with your soul
Be forgiving of your setbacks
Be understanding as you always are.

Say yes to challenges
Say yes to freedom
Say yes to life
Say yes to you.

Numb.

Being frozen became an accustomed state.
The solid cold rushing down my body.
Somehow comfortable and yet I yearned to wriggle free.
Ensnared in a sensation that was both home and prison.
Exchanging minimal dialogue as it required masses of effort.
The long distance cousin of the sleep paralysis demon.
Yet I could move.
I am unchained and hold no restraints.
But hibernation took hold and winter set in.
The scene in between my cracked eyelids began to fade like a closing movie.
The indifferent terror that comes with this sleep.
A gentle cross between floating and falling.
And remaining its submission.
Hollow and heavy - a myriad of contradictions.
But I let it be.
Or did I have no choice?
The soft sharpened slumber takes me in.
I wonder if I'll return this time.

Assistance.

No magic wands he'd say to me,
No spells to help when I can't breathe.
No potion concoction to ease the pain,
No puffs of smoke when I feel insane.

You can grasp at straws, claw at others,
Depend on them like obsessed lovers.
But continued descent will be the result,
Until that power within you can sustain revolt.

OCD And Me.

Same record playing again
in my head.
Trying to find the off button
but to no avail.
Seems like it'll have to be today's
theme music once again.
Let out a disappointed-but-not-surprised
sigh.
Attempt to ignore deafening ache
between my ears.
The one only I can hear.
Still can't figure out how to turn it off,
we carry on.
Pick up a glass, water fills it,
drink.
Put it down.
Pick it up. Put it down.
Pick it up.
Put it down. Stop. Move away.
Okay now I can go.
Exit the area.
Then a cloud out of hiding, shadows
over my head.
I freeze mid motion like a robot who's
battery just died.
Dread fills my being.
Something doesn't feel right. What?
"Did I repeat that enough? Did I touch it properly? Did I neutralise those thoughts correctly? Did I forget
something?"
Like boiling milk, the bubbles
under the surface begin to rise.
Would I get to the
stove in time to stop it ruining
the hob?
Or will my anxiety completely boil up
and blanket over onto the
floor?
A choice presents
itself then.
Much like every move I make.
Everything I touch.

Every thought I think.
To go back or not to go -
that is the question.
Even Willy Shakespeare
can't lessen the
turmoil of this moment.
Do I
Don't I
Back
Forth
This way
That.
That records still playing.
Now heavy percussions
entered.
Cymbals crash
Drums beat down
4 additional tracks have
been added.
Now it's a completely
unharmonious
out of sync
chaotic
disarray of obnoxious screaming illegible chatter.
Before I knew it
I find myself at the glass again.
"Just once" was my mantra.
We all know that
didn't happen.
One turns into 5.
Then a wave poured over me.
Down came the volume.
Somehow managed
to only have minor spillage to the stove.
The tide pulled back
into a dangerous but not
critical level.
But at what cost?
The reinforcement of
illogical behaviour
and beliefs.
Digging
deeper into the groove of
a nasty habit.

"But at least I feel
safe now right?"
Momentarily. Until
the next time.
Like a contraction.
Seconds or minutes apart
and we play this game
all over
again.

Versus.

Variations without explanation
Continued cycles, losing patience
Not to mention - utter frustration
Finding yourself in the same position.
Don't create another addition
The way this is needs no assistance
But I must offer a confession
All I want is your salvation.
Waiting always for some revelation
Wondering ever to reach destination
Happiness, sanity - complete deprivation
Feeling anxiety increase escalation.
Breathing stuck - do I need ventilation?
Sit down, reflect, engage meditation
Yet continue to give in to temptation
Simply reinforcing my bad reputation.
Holding onto control of position
Slow steps towards realisation
A life of freedom awaits with elation
Turns out I was the only solution.

Not An Old Friend.

It could have been so easy
The thing you came to do
At least the above statement is true
Because it proved far from breezy.

A broken record player stuck on loop
Scrambling to find the mains
But even unplugging of power didn't unplug the pain
Grasping at something that'll soothe.

It makes so much sense
And yet is the hardest to execute
To others it seems like just another excuse
Intelligent you are but appearing dense.

But they can't feel the difficulty inside
The frustration where irrationality lies
The endless asking of questions - why
Why is this the hardest goodbye?

Paths.

Eyes are the window to the soul they say,
But I hesitate to let you look amongst the disarray.
Almost like inventions of projected images on the ground,
Though panic quickly ensues, all just remains safe and sound.

Step forward and sir down with nothing but fluid motion,
Knowing there isn't another way to do this but alone - no potion.
See what's here, not was or were,
Just let it fade; be nothing but a blur.

Blame.

Hard to say what caused the pain,
What drove me to feeling insane,
The thing that showers me in shame,
At least I won't do it again,
Total destruction my heads inflamed,
Yet you stand with all your fame,
Each step like the whip of a cane,
Tell me - Who's really to blame?

Challenges.

You have to test yourself they say,
But this game is not one I want to play.
Mind out humps don't cause you to stagger,
When the reality is you are your only hazard.

Hidden in plain sight.

She looked at her perplexed and
couldn't understand why.
Because all they'd ever been taught
Was what the eye could see,

"Mummy, why do you need to take it?"
"Because sometimes darling, the brain gets sick too"

A Façade.

You were nothing more than habit
Addiction.
A fairytale hiding brutal fiction

A Blood Test.

All it was was a queue,
Why was I so afraid
Maybe because I thought it was true
The theories my thoughts made.

Why couldn't I appreciate the day,
Gentle breeze and sunlight on me for once
Every step filled me with dismay
To passers by, what a stupid dance.

Passing too quick but not quick enough,
You insist on making it complicated.
One eye constantly on the ticking clock,
A switch of a second and all laughter is faded.

All it was was a line,
I knew it was something I'd avoid forever
Supportive voice knew I'd be fine
A simple task yet another endeavour.

Angel.

Though I never looked inside your eyes,
I see your reflection in my mind,
I attempt to block you out - I try,
Because you are just an angel in disguise.

Interference.

There again with static picture,
A high-pitched muffled groan,
Blurred pixels and computing errors,
Taking a step back because it didn't like your tone.

A speed bump that grows longer,
A dead end to a dark alley,
Straight jacket suffocation,
Conveyor belt steaming but you move slowly.

Two fingers either end of a trap,
Defence against a netted goal,
A deependinh chasm and no bridge across,
Yet despite that on your travels be a troll.

Which way you step, both move in unison,
High metal gates encircled with barbed wire,
A faulty alarm system disrupts unnecessarily,
Don't allow it to block you - be the fire.

Watching.

Why is it you don't listen when I speak.
I give you direction and route yet you still end up lost.
I try to stay firm with you and you break me down.

What is more clear than the instructions told.
I still get entangled with you each time.
One of us has to be silent,
But which will retreat?

How is it you can be both types of matter simultaneously.
I observe the familiar and watch them run riot.
Still somehow convinced of the irrational.

You surely do not say my words.
But yet you live amongst.
How can I turn away with ignorance when you scream to be heard.
To be blind when horror flashes.

Is it as simple as being two things apart from each other,
And why you bark is my own doing.
If I just stop feeding you another will I finally see the reality of knowing.

A helping hand.

I don't have all the answers.
But maybe a piece of my puzzle is the one you're missing.
So i'll share my words - if it increases the chances,
It helps to find the solutions you're chasing.

Future musings.

Familiarity was both a comfort and fear,
The same old positions perhaps occasionally deferring.
Once something so distant and blurry now so near,
Every pressurising possibility - just scattered images whirring.

Numbers had always meant a lot,
But why is it these crucial ones get ignored?
Seeming logic adding two and two but presents a block,
And how everything around is pushing you to be implored.

Will we finally, after millennials, do what is needed?
Surely the stagnation of current methods screams?
Removing another piece of paper - another year repeated.
Is it not time to realise, you can live the life of your dreams?

Paradox.

I stumbled through the darkness,
Attempts to grasp at light,
Embarrassed at my unsteadiness,
An invisible opponent to fight.

Despite laying my feet on solid ground,
I see a broken walkway beneath,
To shake from delusion - not allowed,
Embedded programming i need to delete.

Moments of reality flicker through,
Behind opaque glasses my eyes cannot see what is
Truly true,
Leaving them smashed on the floor below is where
Truth lies.

But How?

How is it so good yet so bad,
Considered wrong despite the fun had.
How something so freeing becomes a trap,
Now just inevitably falling back.

How is it kept around for this long,
Even when it's obviously wrong.
How can something so stupid be so smart,
Constantly demanding the precision of a dart.

How is it a line hasn't been drawn,
Why can't you lean the other way whilst torn.
How do you tolerate this thing so vile,
Seems it's almost become part of your style.

How is it you ignore the reality you create,
And bloody well realise you control your fate.
How can all this evidence stack up,
And yet you walk around with your eyes shut.

How is it the depression has not lead you through,
It's trying to push you towards what is true.
How can you spill it out and know you're right,
Whilst continuing to allow yourself to lose this fight.

Paper.

You took me in your hands
Cut me up, scrunched me up
Tore through me like paper.
You didn't realise that paper dolls
Have feelings too.

A Girl On Fire.

There's a reason light penetrates through.
Why the darkest room can be thrust into vividness.
If only you knew and could see your likeness.
My oh the wonderful things you'd do.

Tiny glimmers enter tear drops,
Even when encased in emotion - your soul shines.
But to hold such as true shall be a climb,
And it'll have to be done through stomach in knots.

Throw a cigarette butt into a pile of books,
How the smallest of forces becomes an inferno.
And it all starts with the dimmest glow,
Simply enter your heart and take a look.

Once you acquire such knowledge - you are unstoppable.
But then again; you always were.
Only it was all hidden behind an opaque blur,
Having a fire like yours will cause some trouble.

Pawn.

I was powerless beneath your grasp
Suffocation took hold.
Underneath a jagged edged clasp
The story I carry till I'm old.
Your voice broke through me
I'm torn
Whilst you had fun moving me
Around like a pawn.

Useless.

No matter what I do
No matter what I did
You made me feel like I was
Nothing to contend with.
With endless actions
Endless love
I still wasn't enough.
Your ongoing torment was
Ruthless
You labelled me
Utterly
useless.

/

With each passing day
I see a light
One that took much fight
Sometimes i have no words to say.
But i remember the darkness
I remember the pain
Occasionally i feel the same
Feeling utterly hopeless.
But I carry on
Although I feel wrong
Ploughing through
My thoughts aren't true.

Seeing Truth.

You would see the wonders, but never of eye,
Every engaging part of happiness and life,
Feeling powerless, exhausted, unable to try,
But you know this place of mind will not suffice.

Questioning the differences and similarities,
Hard to imagine they had once been in the dark,
Being in complete control - no barriers,
It can be just that; take a walk in a park.

Keep your hope and keep on going,
You're only here once, don't let age escape you,
Maybe you are capable without even knowing,
The voice of lies, nothing will ever be, so don't do.

Smile.

Isn't it funny; the idea of laughter,
Uneven breathing creates such a joy,
Maybe a picture or an old beloved toy,
Time - ever going only seems to move faster.

Happiness is engrained though it can change,
Events and thoughts can make a difference,
But only with positivity can one go the distance,
Aesthetically pleasing, but scientifically strange.

A smile can hide a thousand emotions,
A smile can produce a glimmer of light,
A smile can hold you when you have no fight,
Your smile can fix me when I'm broken.

The hidden observer.

Twas not long before it became a familiar place,
It held the seasons of the world in its hands,
At once - in a moment - an ever changing pace,
Where nothing is real beyond this fenced land.

Awaking to its welcome light; beams streaking in,
Returning again the same spot you'd always been,
To venture as far would be a great sin,
But still you wonder - behind the crystal screen.

A cell of sorts, but a freedom from the dark,
Passing shadows and smiles and cries,
Imagining the etching of names into bark,
Fresh cool air, breeze, a desperate lie.

But at the end of day; what a solemn time,
Nothing but you, space and the distant wind chime.

Yin and Yang.

What gives us the right to name it as so?
It will make the most dull embers glow,
Giving its reputation - just pure isolation,
But the world is nothing without its creation.
Frightening to some and comfort to others,
Under its swallowing grip; becoming smothered,
Constant whispers, howls and screams,
An empty chasm to all of your dreams.

A second to be; a second to be not,
Bringing all feelings into a knot,
Providing the contrast of night and day,
Its beauty is not given as it may.

To hold a paradise or to hold a nightmare?
A place for solitude or a place to share?
Its presence known, but not always wanted,
Turning a wrong direction, being endlessly haunted.

Your brain.

Remember that nothing that's said is true,
That all you get is feeling blue,
Remember that it's just circuitry,
That its only wires crossing into a messy knot.

Remember what it feels to do as you want,
To not let the lies scare and taunt,
Remember that things don't work that way,
That it's just an anxiety rush.

Remember that walking away is best,
That its whats right; despite the pain in your chest,
Remember all the times you did and was real,
Those moments when you could truly see.

Remember that life is only yours,
That you control where you soar,
Remember to ignore and remember to fight,
Trust in reality and watch the fire ignite.

Now.

Caught between two conflicting roads,
One way of liberation; one way of fear,
Constantly worrying, questioning what is known,
Don't let yourself shed a tear.

What is different between you and them?
A simple logical explanation is true,
You want to do these things - but when?
The more you think; the more time you lose.

Seen what is real yet the fear remains,
Convincing your panic; it's time to wake up,
Stop allowing the slipping away of your days,
It is a comfort for a second - but is really just pain.

Two and two don't go together,
Trust yourself, trust them and you will see,
Ever changing thoughts like passings of weather,
Just look out and think about the lone tree.

It has to change, it cannot be and then gone,
Keep your eyes set on everything you've learned,
You know what's being done is nothing but wrong,
Just remove it, it's not needed, let it burn.

A debate.

What is me and what is you,
Constant statements; are they true,
Do you decide or do i,
Everyday kills me inside.

Destroying happiness, removing life,
Bleeding me out like a cut of a knife,
You give me safety yet youre edging me to death,
When I'm contained under you, I struggle for breath.

Why can't i just step on and feel okay,
Falling deeper everyday,
You want to pull me down, why do i give in,
To dismiss your instructions feels like sin.

You promise the world; you hand it to me slow,
But you snatch it sway, you make it a show,
One second of peace but it comes again,
When will these mental nightmares end?

I try to reason, i try to plead,
With every second; im brought to my knees,
You stand and laugh, then offer a hand,
It's slippery, I grasp it, back to land.

Calling me back, did i do it right?
I try to not listen and walk with all my might,
You know how to scare, you know how to taunt,
I can't do this and have the life I want.

Just a first step, sudden blast of icy air,
"Don't worry you can do this" it doesn't seem fair,
Nothing will happen, let go and see,
It's not real, it never will be, it's only anxiety.

Precious aroma.

A delicate touch of sweetness and air,
Pure and crisp; a light cloud,
A feature nothing can compare,
A recogniseable mark in a messy crowd.

Empty rooms give into its embrace,
A trail of happiness and wisdom,
Like smoke of a fire - leaving its trace,
Once present it cannot be undone.

Evoking memories and releasing comfort,
A familiar scent to not be repeated,
You get an image of her; even for a moment,
A sacred possession that can't be deleted.

The journey.

Closed, dark, shut and tight.
Locked, covered, burnt, out of light.
Open, free, luminous, and true.
Revealed, exposed, untouched, new.

Uphill, goals, success and you.
Downwards, spiral, abyss, you.
Reflections, memory, thoughts and love.
Nightmares, heartache, worthless, not enough.

Falling, tumbling, messy and unravelled.
Pathways, roads, location, travels.
Unknown, distant, apart and torn.
Confliction, indifference, ending, dawn.

Clouds, nature, life and breath.
Encased, held, submerged, indepth.
Focus, drive, vision and goals.
Mystery, dreams, unknown, to be held.

Shutting down, endings, keys and secrets.
Dirt, comfort, quiet, trickles.
Always, never, silence and still.
What was, what wasn't, is it even real?

Prevention.

A spark turned into a roaring inferno,
The dwindling of sanity, a distant glow.
The possibilities seem endless,
Thoughts, racing, never rests.

A pace beginning to increase,
Like a dog, violently wriggling from its leach,
Remove the thoughts from your mind,
Don't let it dissect the panic up from inside.

Through the looking glass.

I think we'll always argue the colour of the chair,
Whilst i see red you'll see green,
I'm the one that notices that tiny speck of dust on it and just stares,
It's easy to do nothing but internally scream.

But even though i see the deepest red,
I have to trust you - that my eyes see things reversed,
If i don't do this, i may end up dead,
Despite the thoughts that cause me hurt.

Crossrails.

Strange to not take your own advice,
To be convinced that those actions will suffice.

There is no difference, what they can - you can too
But to see, you have to do.

He doesn't work that way, you must believe,
By trusting logic, only then are you undeceived.

Pinky promise.

I know it's dark in there inside your head,
I see the changes in your eyes,
I will sit with you and cry your tears,
And sing the song you thought you wrote.

Rose tinted.

When you can stop the thoughts,
Everything is yours.

Though it is a skill that must be taught,
To get past that place obscured.

You had everything all along,
It just took a while to see past the wrong.

Hammer and nails.

I watch them through bars.
Grasping at hairs on my head to pull out the pain.
Questions roaming of why.
Plans to do and moving closer.
I'm held down again.
Torn between fear and freedom.

Desert dreams.

How does it feel to see all that you see,
Nothing but a mere drop of what's here.

You can roam as you like with no essence of tiring.

It will seem so different once all is clear,

Where you run around free -
Being who you choose to be.

Starry skies.

You don't need to worry about the things gone,
Don't be convinced what you are is not strong,
That time is no longer, never was, never will,
Time will move fast even if you remain still.

You don't need to listen, though thoughts are rife,
It is you, only you, that decides your life.

Perception.

I painted you with gold and silver,
Whilst they saw you through broken glass.
I breathed you in like cool air in winter,
And they diverted the other way fast.

You puzzled yourself - confused you were,
Yet neither them nor i could see the fault,
Perhaps it was all just a blur,
One tastes sugar and the other salt.

To my feelings.

I know you're meant to protect,
But these feelings are not true,
They are not needed.

Don't turn your good = bad,
I'll help you to see the truth,
But you have to help me too.

No option.

Sometimes it takes nothing more than utter inner force.
A fearful reluctance to see past our current thoughts.
Peer through the barbed wire filled smog and look towards
Freedom.

Different surroundings.

Oh, you've been so brave.
No one dare tell you it's easy.
But you've tested this before, and you know the outcomes.
Why do you continue to be afraid, dear one?
Why do you question yourself?
Do you not see with your own eyes,
Despite what your thoughts scream.
You are no different.
You just have to trust.

Lockdown.

I can feel you through electric walls,
Even when the world becomes stalled.
Your presence till fills mu space,
Though you may be miles away.

You cry and im calm -
I seem strange,
Do nothing but remain trapped all day.
Funny thing is, after years this is comfort,
A place to hide when my mind is submerged.

Giving.

It doesn't take much to do this type,
Of human gesture - takes no time.
But what a change you'll come to find,
Results when we're all a little kind.

A Sacrificial Boomerang.

Did you ever stop to think of how you made me bleed?
The shattered glasses, broken windows, curtains in the breeze,
The loveless photos, meaningless messages, heartless actions again,
Is it hard to believe that once upon a time you were my best friend?

Did you ever stop to think of all the times we shared?
The naïvety, the immaturity, the willingness to think you cared,
I'd gladly tear it from my mind, pour it empty once more,
But you'd already done that; watched it cascade to the floor.

Did you ever stop to think of the love I had for you?
The tears in my eyes, the slow music, everything so true,
You took my heart and lead me on into a fiery depth,
Yet I let you take me, I fight for you, until my final breath.

Harsh Goodbyes.

It wasn't the private conversation we'd hoped.
But expectations never were high here.
Conscious of the tone I held.
Conscious of the facade of busyness.
Much like an experiment, a zoo or double mirror.
Voices were raised and tears were shed.
The thing that connects us - cut.

Silence Is King.

Without words you can begin a revolution.
Don't doubt what you know.
The sun will reappear despite the darkness that is now.
There's no time left to sit on the knowledge with ignorance.
You have that key,
It is just entangled and trapped in the tar of fear.

Blame Game.

It's easy to let the white line be drawn,
And hide away from yourself.
To believe that if this is how you were born,
When in fact you select the cards you are dealt.

But how long can fingers be pointed -
Before the reigns are held,
When will your outlook be undistorted,
Rather than collecting dust like books on a shelf.

Do you think you can just stare at time,
Eyes fixed like it wont move,
Shock them, get up and walk away from the scene of the crime,
Show yourself you will not lose.

If you continue to think and simply wait,
You Are observing an endless metronome,
Why carry on with something you hate,
At any moment you can go forth with the truth you've known.

Just as as easy as throwing up an arm,
Where you are and where you go is only your control,
The heart wrenching must be felt before the calm,
Only to do as you wish is within your soul.

A Veiled Window.

What does hope look like?
Is it endless positivity, clouds of glitter and rainbows floating above a stream of light and happiness?
Or is it that last finger hooked on the edge,
The final push on a marathon
And staring at thunderstorms through lace curtains?

Why?

Why is it you block the light,
The one you say you create.
Why is it thato to believe your lies is easy - to take your bait.
Why is it you insist on attention,
Yet it is never near enough.
Why is it that no matter what is done, can it really ever be too much.
Why is it that you pretend to be something like a hero in disguise.
Why is it that everyone else can see beneath your lies.
Why is it that to break from you is described as such a crime.
Why is it that life is going ever so fast in time.
Why is it I know the laws, the rules that we are.
Why is it that despite my knowledge, it seems I can never get too far.
Why is it that I listen to your record and make the same mistakes.
Why is it that I find these habits so difficult to break.
Why is it that I am different, you never have an answer.
Why is it hard for you to accept I am your master.
Why is it that ideas flow and scenarios are thought.
Why is it the next minute, I'm stuck oh so taut.
When is the time now to stop the dreaded pattern.
Now is the moment to know that nothing will ever happen.

You Haven't Aged.

The sensation was strange,
Not much of one at all,
Every aspect of time merged to a pool,
As though null changed - even age.

A black hole presented itself,
Tempting but so deceptive,
Lead to a place no longer wanting to live,
Sanity collecting dust on a shelf.

And yet the pause remains,
Though much has moved forward,
The stillness sees family bored,
But locked down to non-existent chains.

How does one exit into this decade,
Where new life starts,
And clocks tick to forget the past,
Feel the sunlight basking - step out of the shade.

It Named Itself.

I know you're meant to protect,
But these feelings are not true,
They are not needed,
Don't turn your good - bad,
I'll help you to see the truth,
But you have to help me too.

Room Temperature.

I knew it would be hard
But it was harder
Trapped in an airless container
Surrounded by heads and bodies
Yet feeling so alone
The anxiety caused me to
Shake and shiver.
But it wasn't even cold.

By when?

By day I hope
By day I pray
By day I wish to go away.
By night I pray
By night I hope
By night I try to calm the kaleidoscope.
These whirring images are endless collapse
Through a thorn ridden chasm
I can never relax.
By day I fear
By day I hide
By day I cannot control inside.

Please Remain.

All of these days I hold my breath,
Another moment - another test.
I hold on tight around my finger,
Wondering why the pain ever lingers.

I fight the darkness with every ounce i possess,
Though toxic positivity is not something to ingest.
The years pass by like a seconds hand,
Hold tight your faith; or you'll slip through the sand.

With symboled assistance you can move forward,
Reducing the amount you feel tortured.
Even though your mind may be constant disarray,
You'll always have a million reasons to stay.

Printed in Poland
by Amazon Fulfillment
Poland Sp. z o.o., Wrocław